T0358710

EFFECTIVE LEARNING

Effective Learning

A Practical Guide to Improving Memory

By

Chris Dawson
University of Adelaide, Australia

SENSE PUBLISHERS
ROTTERDAM / BOSTON / TAIPEI

A C.I.P. record for this book is available from the Library of Congress.

ISBN 978-90-8790-868-3 (paperback)
ISBN 978-90-8790-869-0 (hardback)
ISBN 978-90-8790-870-6 (e-book)

Published by: Sense Publishers,
P.O. Box 21858, 3001 AW Rotterdam, The Netherlands
http://www.sensepublishers.com

Printed on acid-free paper

For my grandchildren:
Suzannah, Louisa, Jack and Cooper

CONTENTS

Acknowledgements   ix

Foreword   xi

Introduction   1

PART 1. A First Look at Learning   3
What Is Learning?   3
Educational Learning   4
Learning Semantic Knowledge   4
   Lasting Memories   5
   The Structuring Phase   6
      Keys to Strong Memory   6
      Becoming Familiar with Structuring Strategies   7
      Try One at a Time   7
   The Learning Phase   8
      Rote and Meaningful Learning   8
   Types of Learning   9
Learning Skills   9
Emotions and Learning   12

PART 2. Memory – An Overview   13
Where Do Memories Come From?   13
Storing and Retrieving Memories   14
How Your Brain Stores Memories   14
   Short-Term Memory   15
   Long-Term Memory   16
Retrieving Memories – Recognition or Recall   17
Why Do I Forget?   18
Rote or Meaningful   18
Educational Learning – A Flow Chart   19

PART 3. Strategies for Learning and Structuring   21
The Learning Phase   21
   Getting Started   21
   Multiple Repetitions   21

Making Repetition Work Better 22
   By Distributed Practice 22
   By a Practice and Check Cycle 22
The Structuring Phase 23
   Structuring Non-Meaningful Material 24
      Clustering 25
      Acronyms 26
      Acrostics 28
      Rhymes, Chants and Phrases 29
      Visualisations, Associations and Running Links 31
      Pegwords 32
      Method of Place and Journey 33
      Other Strategies 35
In Summary 35
Some Everyday Memory Challenges 36
   Structuring Meaningful Information 38
      SQ3R 40
      Hierarchical Concept Maps 41
      Spider Concept Maps 44
      Mind Maps 45
      Tree Diagrams 46
      Flow Charts 49
      Analogies 50

How to Jog Your Memory 53

A Flow Chart for Learning Decisions 55

Bibliography 57

Index 59

ACKNOWLEDGEMENTS

The embryonic ideas for this guide were collected from a variety of sources in preparation for a Graduate Diploma in Education short course at the University of Adelaide in 2002. I am grateful to those students who, in the next three years, provided me with support and feedback, and convinced me of the potential usefulness of a guide with a focus on learning.

Special thanks to the following for their contributions:

Emma Barson
Sarah Farrelly
Mark McCann
Ryan Mendes
Mark Pompeuse
Virginia Rawlinson
Kath Reynolds
Rebecca Sampson
Matthew Shakeshaft
Kinnari Shelat
Adam Starrs
Tanya Taylor-Cox
Michael Tsouvallas

FOREWORD

The human brain is amazing, and the range of abilities it gives us is vast. Just look at the many different things even a three year old can do, and compare that with the very restricted skills of the most powerful computer.

One aim of education is to develop each student's abilities to the full, and among the abilities it focuses on is the ability to think. This includes the skill of solving relatively straightforward problems, but also the ability to tackle more complex ones where clear answers are not easy to find. To do all of this, students need to learn to think independently, to cooperate with others, and to think both critically and creatively. But, while thinking is supremely important, it is also important to have something to think about. When we think, we draw on knowledge we already have, whether it be knowledge of facts or knowledge of how to do things. Of course, we might need to seek additional knowledge when we tackle a new problem, but we tie that knowledge to things we already know.

In recent years some educational thinkers have tended to devalue learning, on the basis that it is always possible to look up specific knowledge in books or the internet. And it is true that there is no need to remember most things you come across. However in each area of knowledge there is some information, and there are some skills that are fundamental, and needed regularly – and it is worthwhile having them readily available. And, in a more practical vein, students do get tested and examined, and part of the testing will look at what they know, and what they can do with that knowledge. So gaining knowledge is an important part of education.

In saying this, I am not advocating a return to an educational system that focuses its attention totally on students remembering vast amounts of information in a parrot-like way. Balance is needed, and part of that balance is the need to learn some fundamental knowledge and skills. So this guide is designed to provide you with ways to make your learning easier and more efficient.

> It's easy to assume that learning is natural, and that everyone can do it effectively. But the best learning strategies do NOT come naturally.

This guide has a limited focus: its sole aim is to help learners learn more effectively. It is not a comprehensive guide to study skills, though some of its contents will normally be found in books of that type. Upper secondary, and older learners, should be able to work with the guide independently to develop more effective learning approaches. Younger students should also benefit, providing parents, teachers or older learners support them. The guide will be of value to teachers who can incorporate some of the strategies into subject based classroom or homework tasks. In that way, their students can develop specific subject knowledge and general learning strategies at the same time. And several parts of the guide will be useful for anyone who, at any time, needs to remember something – a name, a shopping list, or things to do tomorrow morning.

In the context of the guide, 'learning' means an attempt by a person to take some new material and store it in the brain in such a way that it can be retrieved, and used, when it's needed at a later time. This new material might be unconnected information, such as a list; or it might be meaningful material into which are built links between various ideas or concepts; or it might be a new manipulative or thinking skill. In addition 'learning' also includes the improvement of either existing knowledge or skill.

The motif used throughout this guide is the elephant. Why the elephant? Because it never forgets!

An elephant was walking along the riverbank with his partner when he saw a turtle sunning itself on the mud flat. Walking over to it, he kicked it hard, and it went flying – splat – into the mud on the other side of the river.

"What did you do that for?" said his partner.

"Well", he said, "thirty years ago that turtle bit me on the ankle, and my ankle still hurts from it".

"How do you know it was the same turtle?" asked his partner.

"Turtle recall".

Memory is the primary and fundamental power, without which there could be no other intellectual operation.

Samuel Johnson

Unless we remember we cannot understand.

E.M. Forster

INTRODUCTION

In 2002, 32 competitors in the final of the World Memory Championship memorised lists of numbers, names, quotations, dates, the sequence of shuffled cards and random words.

The winner learned 2 643 random digits in 30 minutes, 1 197 playing cards in an hour and 280 spoken digits in 5 minutes.

Surprisingly, studies of the competitors showed they had no higher intelligence than other people with similar backgrounds. Also, in tasks such as remembering snowflake patterns, they were little better than the comparison group.

The conclusion is that differences in performance between those with fantastic memories and the rest of us comes from the use of special strategies to help memory, and from practice with these strategies on specific tasks.

This guide is not designed to help you recall 1 197 playing cards, or to duplicate any of the memory feats above. Any of these would make a great party trick, but the guide has a more practical aim. Its major focus is on improving memory, mainly in educational settings – that is learning at school, TAFE, university and so on – but also in everyday situations. Some of this learning will involve remembering un-linked information, such as the names of people, or shopping lists, or French vocabulary or scientific names. However, in educational settings it frequently involves learning linked, meaningful and complex information.

The guide aims to help you learn better by providing:

- strategies for structuring new material into a learnable form;
- ways to make learning more efficient.

Ultimately you are responsible for what you learn. Teachers and textbooks can help, but they can only organise material to make learning easier. In the end you have to take the decisions about what you will try to learn, and how you will go about it.

The guide is presented in three main parts:

Part 1. A first look at learning

This provides an overview of how we learn, and of different sorts of learning. This part should be read before you look at other parts.

Part 2. Memory – an overview

An account of how the brain seems to go about learning. While it is not absolutely necessary for you to read this, you might find some keys to help you better understand some of your own abilities, or lack of them – such as "Why do I seem to forget so quickly?"

Part 3. Strategies for learning and structuring

Here, tested structuring strategies, and effective learning approaches, for both non-meaningful and meaningful learning are described, and illustrated by examples. Once you are familiar with some of these strategies, whenever you start to learn something new you will be able to select a learning approach that is most likely to work for you.

Interspersed throughout the guide are a number of quotes which illustrate some of the strengths and weaknesses of our memories.

Memory is the diary that we all carry about with us

     Oscar Wilde

PART 1. A FIRST LOOK AT LEARNING

WHAT IS LEARNING?

Learning means either gaining some new knowledge or a new skill, or getting better at something. Learning can be focussed on something which is commonplace, such as remembering a shopping list, or the things we need to do this afternoon. Or it might involve learning a new recreational skill, such as how to complete a Su Doku puzzle, cook an omelette, or play a backhand tennis volley.

Learning in educational institutions is specifically tied to particular teaching subjects. Learners might be trying to remember some Japanese vocabulary, a poem, or a definition. Or they could be learning how to calculate the answer to a problem, use a burette, play a piece of music, discuss a political issue, conduct a scientific experiment, or evaluate a newspaper advertisement. And so on.

In all of these, to effectively learn a new ability, or to improve on an existing ability, learners must:

---

1. pay attention to what they intend to learn (or improve);
2. store the new learning at some place in the brain (that is memorise it);
3. retrieve the learned material when it is needed at a later time;
4. use the retrieved memory in some sort of action.

This is seen in the following diagram:

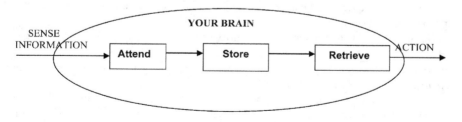

This means remembering is not easy, because it can go wrong at any of these stages. So any effective approach to memorising must take into account the best ways of handling all these steps.

EDUCATIONAL LEARNING

Learning in educational institutions is largely characterised by having someone other than the learner, such as a teacher or curriculum writer, decide what is to be learned. To an extent, they also decide how the learner should go about it. This contrasts with personal learning where the learner chooses to learn something because of a special interest.

There are two main types of knowledge learned in educational settings, *semantic* and *procedural*. Semantic knowledge is what we usually call "knowledge". It is the sort found in written or diagrammatic form in school textbooks. Facts, theories and so on are all part of semantic knowledge. If someone asks you whether you know something, and you can show it by speaking it, writing it, or drawing a diagram of it, then you are accessing semantic knowledge.

Procedural knowledge is skill knowledge or "doing knowledge". Tying your shoelaces, drinking from a cup, operating a forklift truck, skiing, lighting a Bunsen burner, playing a musical piece, and solving long division problems are all examples of procedural knowledge. It is possible for a person to be able to talk sensibly about how to ski (semantic knowledge) and to be able to ski (skill knowledge), but it is also possible to be able to do one and not the other.

Schools are concerned with both semantic and skill knowledge, and there are some similarities in how they are learned – but there are also differences. In this guide the two are separated.

LEARNING SEMANTIC KNOWLEDGE

Different learners will often tackle learning the same material in different ways. For instance, when time is short, and there is no interest in the topic, one learner might simply try to memorise the material just to pass an upcoming test. With more time available, and an interest in the material, a different learner will adopt strategies to gain a deep understanding. At the heart of this is the *choice* on the part of the learner – it is much better to choose a strategy that suits you at the time, rather than to use the same strategy all the time, whatever the material or the conditions. However you also need to be aware of the potential strengths and limitations of the approach you choose.

Some key points about semantic memory are:

Remembering something takes effort
> Most memories don't just happen. If you want to learn something well, you have to work at it.

Linked information is easier to learn
> Material that is linked, within itself or to other information, is more easily remembered than isolated bits of information.

Forgetting is normal, but under some conditions forgetting is faster
We all forget, but some things are forgotten faster than others. Effective strategies can speed learning and slow forgetting.

You can't forget what you never learned
Sometimes, when people say they've forgotten something, they hadn't really learned it well in the first place, so it's not surprising they don't remember it.

Using tested approaches to memorising can help us all learn better
And that's what this guide is about.

Lasting Memories

Stable memories, or those which are to last a long time, must be stored in long-term memory (LTM) in the brain. And the best single hint for making that happen is to *create links*. The more links to other memories, the more firmly a memory is stabilised, and the more easily it can be retrieved and used. Appropriate links are already built into much educational material, but for other material they have to be created.

Let us look at a simple process of creating links from within a list. Assume we have to learn the following biological classification, which takes us from the most inclusive to the least (the single species):

Kingdom
Phylum
Class
Order
Family
Genus
Species

How do we go about learning it? Obviously we can repeat it to ourselves over and over. Soon we may think we know the classification, but may be a little afraid we will get the order wrong. So, using the first letter in each word, we create a device (called an acrostic) to link the order to something else we can easily remember. There is one possibility below, but making your own can be more effective – and more fun!

Kooky Professors Can Organise Fantastically Great Science.

This artificial aid assists memory and its accurate recall. Think of how you remember the colours of the rainbow in their correct order. Most of us use something like: ROY G BIV or Richard of York Gave Battle in Vain.

In a similar way, assume you need to learn this drawing:

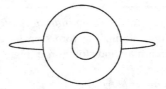

You could try to imagine the whole picture in your mind, and practise thinking about it. But more often you will try to organise it in your mind by noting it consists of a large circle with a smaller one inside it, then there is bit that sticks out at each side. Or you can go further and say that it's a bird's eye view of a Mexican on a bicycle (look at it – see what I mean!). In either of the last two approaches, you are preparing to learn more efficiently by making links to what you already know.

All learning is more effective if the learner prepares in this way. Where links already exist in the material to be learned (*meaningful material*), we need to make full use of them. Where they don't exist (*non-meaningful material*), we can create some.

Notice that when attempting to learn any new semantic knowledge, there are two phases. First, there is a *structuring* step that either brings together all the potential links existing in the material or, if necessary, creates new links for the purpose. Then this is followed by the actual *learning* step where repetition of the material will be involved in some way.

In this guide, these are termed:

- *The Structuring Phase*
- *The Learning Phase*

Both of these are needed for effective learning. However it is possible to avoid the first, and simply try to learn any sort of material by repetition, with no thought being given to structuring. That sort of learning is very common, but of limited long-term value.

In Part 3 of this guide, these two phases are discussed separately, with the focus being on actual strategies, and examples of how they can be used. Here, each phase is introduced briefly so that you will have a general understanding of how learning takes place, and of some of its characteristics and difficulties.

The Structuring Phase

When you decide to try to learn something, the actual learning step will usually be preceded by a structuring phase. In Part 3 strategies for structuring are discussed in detail, but all of them make use of one, or more, of the following keys to strong memory.

Keys to Strong Memory
Memories are strongest, and more easily retrievable, when they have just been created. In time they may weaken, and the material is less easily recalled. However various strengthening tactics, each of which makes use of what the brain is good

at doing, can slow this process of forgetting. These are shown below, and can be remembered using the initial letters CARV (this is called an acronym):

Comprehension As far as possible, make sure you understand the material you are memorising.

Association Make links between different parts of the material you are memorising, and with other knowledge you already have.

Repetition Rehearse what you are memorising a number of times, then undertake additional rehearsals at intervals.

Visualisation Whenever you can, create vivid mental images of what you are learning.

Unfortunately you won't always be able to apply all these tactics when you try to learn something. However, where possible, try to understand the material, and create links (associations) with what you already know. If genuine comprehension is impossible, create artificial associations, and make as much use as possible of visualisation.

> People often ask 'How do you remember so much? Do you have a photographic memory?' I need a combination of context, passion, understanding and application to master new subjects, and I have no special skills for remembering unsympathetic materials, such as random numbers. I never consciously used a memory system and rarely used mnemonics. My success relied on capacity to build up contexts and affinities.
>
> Barry Jones

Becoming Familiar with Structuring Strategies
To become familiar with the different structuring strategies available to you, read through Part 3 quite quickly, looking at strategies for structuring both meaningful and non-meaningful material. Do you use any of them now? Have you found them successful? Do you think any of the other strategies might help you?

Be careful. It's easy to reject something because it's new, or looks a little difficult. Remember, all the strategies are effective, and not too difficult to learn. Of course it will take a little practice to make them useful, but this will pay off because, once learned, they will be available to you for the rest of your life. So investing a bit of time is worthwhile.

Try One at a Time
After reading through all the strategies, your best approach is to select a strategy which looks useful, and which fits reasonably well with what you do now. Next time you have to learn something, try it out. You might find things a little difficult, but persevere. Next time it will be easier. Think about it afterwards – was it effective? Perhaps learning took a little longer than usual. But now you're familiar with the

strategy, it should take less time on the next occasion. And the most important thing is – how well do you remember the material? Is your memory of it better than usual? If so, the process was very worthwhile!

Next time use the same strategy again. It should be easier. Now you should be gaining confidence. Try another strategy and check whether it works. Then practise it with different material. Keep doing this until you add four or five new structuring strategies to your armoury – some for meaningful material, and some for non-meaningful material. Later, you can gradually add more.

The Learning Phase

When the new material has been structured as well as you can do it, the second phase involves the actual learning process. However you will now find this less demanding than you might think, because the process of structuring will have already helped you learn the material quite well.

Rote and Meaningful Learning

Rote learning relates to learning information so it can be retrieved later in much the same form as it was initially learned. For instance you may wish to remember the capital cities of all the countries in Europe, the names of the brass instruments in an orchestra, the French words for various objects around the house, a poem or a shopping list. While these might all need to be recalled in a specific way, there are no built-in connections between different items, and it's not easy to relate them to any existing knowledge. A common approach to learning this sort of information is to rehearse the material over and over in a mechanical way. However this learning approach can be improved upon, as you will see a little later.

Meaningful learning requires the learner to develop an understanding of the material, where existing links and relationships between different components are identified, and where links might also be made to knowledge the learner already possesses. Thus a historical study of the causes of World War 1, or an understanding of electrical theory, the complex plot of a novel, or the ethical arguments behind a decision to store a DNA profile of new infants, would all require a wide breadth of linked knowledge. A check on the success of this sort of learning doesn't require exact repetition of what was learned. Instead the intention is to see whether learners can use their own words to show understanding of the material, and also whether they can demonstrate its use in solving problems, or in tackling new types of tasks.

Strictly speaking, the rote-meaningful distinction refers to a scale:

Rote  Meaningful

Very few things will be learned with no sort of understanding at all – that is at the extreme rote end. But for many ideas, the extent of understanding can begin in a very small way, and increase with time and experience. So the meaningful understanding of new material is often highly extendable. For instance the simple notions of space and time we all are familiar with can eventually be taken forward to an understanding of Einstein's space-time dimension.

Types of Learning

Any semantic material you start to learn is characterised by being potentially meaningful or not. That is, it may have built-in links which you can look for and develop to make it meaningful, or it may have no such links. If there are no links, then the material can only be learned by simple repetition, unless you can create artificial links to help memory and its retrieval. If there are potential links, then you have a choice. You can choose to identify them, and incorporate them into one or more of the structuring strategies appropriate for meaningful material from Part 3, or you can choose not to do this, and simply adopt a repetitive approach. When making this choice, you might think that the meaningful approach will take longer because you first have to understand the material, and then structure it, and then learn it. Instead, you might feel that you would just like to get down to the learning. However it is important to realise that the time spent in developing the meaning of material is paid back dramatically in the overall efficiency of the learning that occurs.

The flowchart summarises the choices you have to make when you start to learn something new.

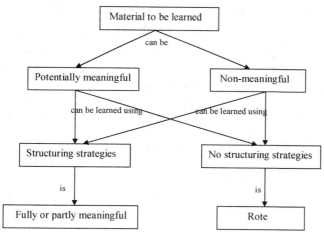

Don't forget. Where possible . . .

First structure

Then learn

LEARNING SKILLS

Unlike semantic learning, where you demonstrate your learning by talking or writing about something, skill or procedural learning is demonstrated by successful actions. So a skilled typist demonstrates her procedural knowledge by typing rapidly and accurately. However, when asked, she might not be able to say where X or B is on the keyboard. Her fingers appear to know (skill knowledge), but her brain may not (semantic knowledge). Procedural knowledge includes physical

9

skills (such as writing, or riding a bicycle), and also some problem solving skills, habits and so on.

There are four important stages when learning procedural skills:

> 1. The skill is demonstrated by someone, and what is required is explained to the learners, after which they may talk about it to clarify (Novice).
> 2. Each learner then begins to practise the skill, gradually recognising and correcting errors (Beginner).
> 3. The learner becomes more skilled, with speed and accuracy improving (Competent, then Proficient).
> 4. The learner is able to reflect on the skill and to modify it to meet changing conditions (Expert).

Practice is vital in procedural learning. Because skills take more learning than semantic knowledge, they must be practised many times. However, once fixed, they can be almost permanent (once you can ride a bicycle, you can always ride a bicycle), so the effort is worthwhile. Combined with practice is the need for clear and helpful feedback on performance. This feedback can come in different ways – from the task, or from other people. You know if you are failing to ride your bicycle, but you might have to be told that you are making errors in a group of mathematical problems. This need for feedback is why even world-class golfers and tennis players still employ coaches. If their skill level does slip a little, it can usually be corrected when the current performance is compared with the ideal, and the differences, or errors, are made obvious and are attended to. (See the first section in Part 3 for how to best use repetition and practice.)

> Practice doesn't make perfect. Only perfect practice makes perfect.

Even though you might be able to perform them extremely well, procedural skills can be difficult to talk about to others. For instance, riding a bicycle is an example of procedural knowledge, however it is challenging to explain to someone exactly how you do it. And trying this while riding can end in disaster! Similarly, some teachers are good at solving problems, but not so good at explaining to students how they do it.

Many skills are composites of several simpler skills. When learning to drive a car, there are so many different skills to focus on (steering, braking, watching road conditions etc.) that the beginner wonders how it is all possible. But, with practice, the individual skills are improved, and eventually they merge together into a single "car-driving" skill. The same can be said about other skills, such as the ability to solve a particular type of mathematics problem. Again this usually involves the joining of other sub-skills, which you have learned earlier, into a new and specific skill for that type of problem.

Both manipulative and thinking skills that are performed regularly eventually become routine. Because they can now be done easily and automatically, more brainpower is made available for any particularly difficult, or unexpected, parts of the task. You don't have to focus your attention on getting the skill right.

Developing complex procedural skills to expert level needs a massive amount of practice. Chess grand masters can only play 25 simultaneous chess games blindfolded because they have played chess for thousands and thousands of hours. As William G. Chase of Carnegie Mellon University said about developing expertise:

> "No pain, no gain."

Skill knowledge often combines with semantic knowledge. Following constant repetition of, say, simple division calculations, most students will be able to solve them in a test. However, they may not be able to explain how the method actually solves the problem. But it is that sort of meaningful semantic learning that is needed if a student is to progress well in mathematics – or in any other subject area. In the same way, a golf professional doesn't just hit the ball, she also feels (procedural) and knows (semantic) what the implications are of making slight changes to her stance or grip.

A flowchart for procedural learning is shown below.

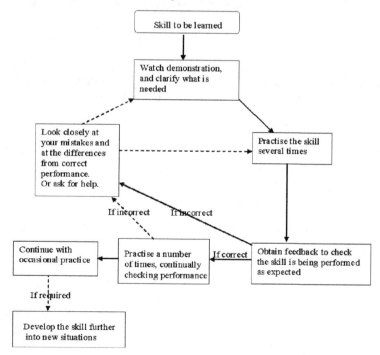

EMOTIONS AND LEARNING

The experiences we have when we are under emotional pressure are usually remembered well. For instance, those of us who are old enough remember exactly where we were when John F. Kennedy was assassinated. More recently, the emotions raised at the death of Princess Diana fixed images in our minds that may never be erased.

> What we learn with pleasure we never forget.
>
> Alfred Mercier
>
> No one is likely to remember what is entirely uninteresting to him.
>
> George MacDonald

So, try to enjoy your learning. Feel good about your successes, and don't worry excessively about your failures.

Now go to: $\Longrightarrow$

Part 2.
To gain a deeper understanding of how your memory works

or

Part 3.
For a detailed look at effective learning and structuring strategies for both non-meaningful and meaningful learning.

PART 2. MEMORY – AN OVERVIEW

Learning is natural; we all do it, and all of us are good learners. Just think of all the things you know, and of all the things you have learned to do.

Some people say they can't learn. This isn't true; we are learning all the time. And there is no end to it. Don't worry – there is no danger of overfilling the brain.

Of course, some of us are better at remembering than others, though often people who appear to have a superior memory can only demonstrate it in one context. For instance, chess grandmasters have an excellent memory of a chessboard part-way through a game, but their memory is little better than anyone else's if the pieces are place randomly. Their good memory is a result of many, many hours of playing real games.

Surprisingly, a fantastic memory is not necessarily a good thing. In Borges' fictional story, *Funes the memorious*. Funes remembers everything in isolation. A dog seen sideways is a different event from the same dog seen front on. A different dog is different again – so no general idea of "dogness" (i.e. the concept of 'dog') develops. And no experience is forgotten. For Funes, every detail is remembered, and he is almost incapable of thought. His memory consists only of thousands and thousands of individual pieces.

That sort of memory is very different from our normal experience where we remember many details for a little while, but gradually, if we are left with anything, it is only the core idea. Most of our memory is not concerned with detail, but focusses around concepts (i.e. mental collections of similar things). We don't remember every detail of every individual dog – instead we remember "dogness".

WHERE DO MEMORIES COME FROM?

Our knowledge comes to us by different paths. Some is *innate*, programmed into our genetic makeup. Apart from that, everything else we know comes through our many different life experiences. A large part of this is from *incidental* learning. For instance we learn to speak and understand largely in informal situations, not because parents sit us down at a desk and teach us. And much of what we learn and remember every day is generated within similar, non-formal settings where we simply experience the world and people around us.

Other learning is *intentional*. You may decide to learn about something that interests you (I've just started to learn how to attack Su Doku puzzles). You go to books or the internet, or talk to people, or simply try to do something new. You direct the search, looking for what you need, finding information to fill gaps, and so on. Here the learning is structured, but you are in control of what you want to find out, and how you go about it – and you also decide when to stop.

But, for the most part, *educational* learning is different. It is characterised by teachers or syllabuses specifying what is to be learned, how you will go about it, how your learning will be assessed, and so on. So, in an educational setting, you will be involved in the study of a range of different subjects, some of which will interest you, but some of which won't.

STORING AND RETRIEVING MEMORIES

While knowledge resides in the head of the learner, the only way it can be detected by others (such as a teacher) is for the learner to demonstrate its use. The change in your knowledge makes possible a change in behaviour. That is, after learning something new, a learner can do something she couldn't do before. So the aim of educational learning is to get the learner to a point where she can demonstrate her learning by performing a new type of action, or showing improvement in an old action. And this explains why teachers and lecturers set tests, essays, projects, practical exercises, etc., to check on what has been learned.

HOW YOUR BRAIN STORES MEMORIES

While a great deal is known about how the brain works, there is still much to find out, and there is debate about even some apparently simpler aspects. A reasonably current overview is given here.

Three basic types of memory stores have been distinguished: sensory memory, short-term memory (STM) and long-term memory (LTM). New learning involves new information being picked up by one of the five senses and transferred into *sensory memory*. Most of the information available to the senses is ignored (think of all the different things your eyes, ears, etc., could be picking up at this moment that you could attend to if you wanted – but instead you are focussing totally on this book – aren't you?). In other words, only a small part of incoming sensory information is selected for further processing.

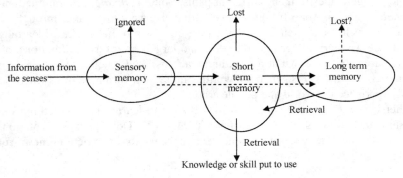

An early view was that all information selected for further processing was passed directly from sensory memory into a short-term memory store, however that view may be an over simplification of what actually can occur. Much information takes this route, but other information can go straight into long-term memory.

Short-Term Memory

Currently STM is considered to be a memory store that takes care of at least four separate functions.

First there is *immediate memory*. This is able to hold the current stream of thought and its information for up to about 30 seconds. So this allows us to listen to someone speaking, continuously linking what has just been said with what is being uttered right now.

Secondly, *working memory* assists in holding information in STM through a rehearsal process. Here stored memories are continuously, and rapidly, replayed so they are kept in mind. This allows us to work on problems where we have to draw several bits of knowledge together.

Because working memory essentially involves rehearsal, and rehearsal requires the repeated review of what is stored, its capacity is limited – it is normally between five and nine (depending on the person) separate bits of information. For instance, when we work through a mathematics problem, we usually have to keep several bits of information in the mind at the same time, so they can be compared and manipulated mathematically. And we know that there are limits to how much we can handle, and that sometimes our brains feel like they are about to burst with all the different bits of information we are trying to work with. At this point, we have reached the capacity of working memory. It's like a juggler trying to keep a number of balls in the air. As he keeps adding to the number, it gets more and more difficult until he reaches his limit and drops them all.

However, if the juggler could stick all the balls together, he would find it much easier. It's the same with the demands on working memory. The capacity of working memory can frequently be increased by the prior *chunking* of information. Several isolated bits of information are first put together, then worked with as a whole, that is as a single piece of information.

To see the effect of chunking, look at the two sequences of 12 letters below. Which would be easier to remember?

xyflsqpkbnwd

fishandchips

The second is easier because it can be stored as a single item. Of course, if you had never heard of fish and chips, or if you were Chinese, and couldn't read English, the demands of the second task could be as great as the first. Chunking is particularly important in the learning of procedural knowledge, where new component skills are practised separately, then linked together into a single skill, such as the ability to ski.

The third component of STM is a *temporary store* where information can be held for up to about an hour without being actively processed during that time. This means something you experienced up to an hour ago might be remembered well, however it will then fade quickly unless it is rehearsed, or transferred to LTM. (One advantage of this store is that it allows you to make last minute memory gains as you sit on the steps waiting for the examination room to open!)

The final *control* component manages the interaction between the different parts of STM, and the links to both sensory and long-term memories. It is involved in the selection of what is put into STM, how it is processed, and what happens to it next.

Long-Term Memory

Long-term memory is the main store of stable memories. It is characterised by the vast amounts of memories it can hold, and by the fact that its memories are retained for weeks, years or decades. When needed, its memories are shifted to the short-term memory system for actual use. Long-term memory can be classified in different ways; one way is to list the different types of content it can hold.

- *Declarative memory* refers to the storage of information that can be consciously brought to mind and talked about (i.e. we can declare it). It includes:
  - *Autobiographical memory*: memory about oneself, and about our experiences in the past, including details of time and place (memory of experiences is also called *episodic memory*). So you probably remember very clearly what happened, when it happened, and where it happened, at the party last Saturday night. You might also remember some incidents of the last holiday you took quite well. Episodic memory is very detailed immediately after an event, but the details quickly fade and only the significant core of a limited number of events remains.
  - *Semantic memory*: our knowledge and understanding of the world, e.g. facts, concepts and theories.

- *Non-declarative memory* relates to knowledge we usually draw on unconsciously – that is we don't think about it as we use it. It includes a range of skills, habits and emotional responses. From an educational point of view, procedural memory, that is the memory of how to do certain things, is the most important.
  - *Procedural memory*. This includes all the motor skills we use, such as using a knife and fork, tying our shoelaces, or playing the piano. It also includes cognitive skills (or mental skills), such as the ability to read, or to solve specific problems in mathematics, or to design an experiment in science.

You will know from experience that declarative and non-declarative memories of the same thing can be separate from each other, or joined. For instance, some people are able to play a piano piece after hearing it once, yet they know nothing about music theory. Others might understand the theory, without being able to perform. However, often these different memory types are interrelated. So we might use a skill totally unconsciously yet, if asked, we can talk about it. For instance, many people can successfully drive a car for quite long periods without much conscious thought, and yet it is also possible to tell someone what is being done at each moment, and why. Similarly, after a lot of practice, a learner can complete long division calculations automatically. However, if asked, she might also be able to explain what she is doing, and why. In these cases, semantic and skill memories are both available.

RETRIEVING MEMORIES – RECOGNITION OR RECALL

Being able to retrieve a memory from LTM when it is needed is vital. This retrieval can be initiated in two ways, through *recognition* or *recall*. You are introduced to someone at a party and later, when you see that person on the street, you know that you have seen the person before – you recognise her. But you can't recall her name. However, if you are told it again, you recognise it from earlier.

Retrieval through the triggering mechanism of recognition can play a part in multiple-choice tests. Four possible answers are provided, and one might be recognised as something you have seen before. The importance of recognition memory can be seen in the TV quiz game *Who Wants To Be a Millionaire?* For instance a contestant was given the question:

> Chartered in 1600 by the English government for trade with Asian countries was the what India Company?

> A. East   B. North   C. South   D. West

The contestant said he didn't know but had heard of East India in some context. After choosing 50/50, only East and North were left and he chose the right one. Without doubt though, if he had been asked the question:

> What company was chartered by the English government in 1600 for trade with Asian countries?

he wouldn't have been unsuccessful. While a memory was there, it was only retrieved as a result of the prompt.

Where retrieval is not prompted by recognition, such as when you need to fill in gaps in sentences, write essays, or answer questions in class, you have to use recall memory. Where information has been learned with meaning, that is with links to many other areas, recall can be assisted through several different pathways. However, at times, recall memory can be very frustrating. An answer may be on the tip of the tongue - you know the answer, it's almost there, but it doesn't come. In cases like this just putting the task on one side, and getting on with something else, may allow retrieval (see 'How to jog your memory' on p. 53).

WHY DO I FORGET?

Though it seems obvious, it's important to recognise that it is impossible to retrieve something from memory if it was never properly remembered in the first place.

Even when memories seem to be stored effectively, they may be forgotten a little later. For instance, one common way of putting information into memory is simply to repeat the information a number of times. This aids memory, though it is not the only approach. Unfortunately, if information memorised in this way is not brought to mind fairly frequently, it can become unavailable (that is you will "forget" it). Indeed forgetting occurs quite rapidly at first, and then slows down. At the end of two weeks or so, there is often little left, though what is still there might be quite well fixed.

Forgetting can be accelerated by a process of *interference*. New learning can interfere with what you knew before, and make you forget it. Or what you knew before can interfere with new learning – and so on. So some things can be forgotten far more quickly than you might expect because of interference from other information – and it's not your fault!

There has been debate about whether forgetting something means it has been totally lost from memory, or whether it is still there and simply can't be retrieved. For our purposes, this debate is irrelevant because, from a student's point of view, if a memory can't be retrieved when needed, it's of no use.

Importantly:

Remembering something to recognition level is relatively easy, but remembering to recall level takes much more effort

Interference can cause forgetting to be faster than usual.

ROTE OR MEANINGFUL

In Part 1 of this guide, a distinction was drawn between rote memory (where the memory is, in effect, a copy of what was learned) and meaningful memory. Rote memory has received bad press in educational circles, and it has been argued that there is no need to overload the mind with specific information. To an extent this is true, however it is usually necessary to create a sound memory of the basic components, whatever the subject you are studying.

There are some things, like the alphabet, which can only be known by rote, and it would be time wasted if you had to look up the alphabet each time you wanted to find a particular word in the dictionary. Similarly biologists need to learn the names of different cell components, medical students the names of the nerves in the human body, history students must know some dates and names, artists should know to mix blue and yellow to produce green, musicians need their scales, and many of us learn some poetry by rote. And the list goes on.

Initially we might first learn our multiplication tables by rote by repeatedly chanting them during primary schooling, and this enables us to reproduce them quickly when needed. However most of us develop a meaningful understanding as well – so we know that 6 piles of 7, and 7 piles of 6, both contain 42 articles. In school it is possible to learn first by rote, and give meaning later. In fact, the rote versus meaningful distinction is not a totally appropriate one to make. Very few things are learned with no meaning at all, and the extent of meaning can be developed over time. One can learn a physics definition of a force with no meaning attached to it. However giving meaning to this – what a force is, and what it is not – can be developed with greater and greater sophistication across many years of a physics education. The meaningful side of the rote–meaningful scale can be highly extendable.

EDUCATIONAL LEARNING – A FLOW CHART

Most learning, whether semantic or procedural, involves the sequence outlined in the diagram below. The initial learning phase is most important, and how a learner tackles that is a matter of choice. Some study guides suggest that all learners should adopt the same approach to learning at all times. However, this guide takes a different view. There are different ways to go about learning (i.e. it can be by rote or meaningfully, and different strategies can be used for each), and it puts the final choices in the hands of the individual.

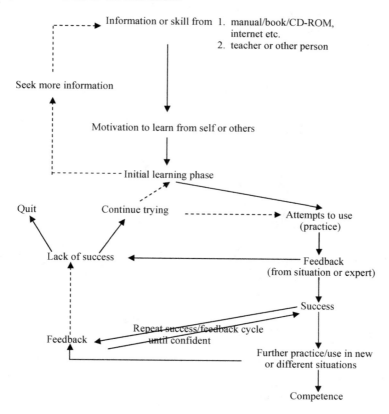

PART 3. STRATEGIES FOR LEARNING AND STRUCTURING

Part 3 focuses on learning semantic material – that is what we usually label as 'knowledge'. Procedural or skill learning, the other major component of educational learning, was covered in Part 1, 'Learning Skills'.

When you start to learn something new, you will usually need to structure the material before you try to learn it. However, here the learning phase is outlined first because it will be used in all your learning, and the approach you take to it will not need to be changed much. The structuring strategies follow.

THE LEARNING PHASE

Getting Started

Effective learning requires effort and commitment – it doesn't just happen. So when you start to learn, whether it's semantic learning or procedural learning, your attention needs to be focused on the task. To get to this point, the first thing to do is to get the conditions right. Prepare by:

- eliminating external distractions such as disturbing noises, or the room being too hot or too cold; and
- fixing up, or putting to one side, internal distractions such as hunger or thirst, or problems in the family.

Now concentrate on the process of learning. The key here is to use some form of repetition to help store the organised material in long-term memory. However you should look carefully at the following discussion of repetition, because simple repetition is not the most effective way of learning.

Effective learners use repetition intelligently

Multiple Repetitions

The strategy for learning by multiple repetitions (or rehearsal) is simple – you read the material, or write it, or say it, or think it, a number of times until you've "got it".

21

Learners commonly use this basic strategy by itself, and without any attempt at prior structuring of the material, especially when they are learning at the last minute (cramming), or when they have no particular interest in the material. However, while this might allow short-term success, memories formed in this way are usually quickly forgotten. So you might pass the test or exam, but you will have to spend time re-learning the material the next time you need it.

Nevertheless some form of repetition is a necessary component of virtually all learning, and it is essential that the repetitive strategy is made as efficient as possible.

Making Repetition Work Better

By Distributed Practice

Whenever you've learned something, the best way to slow forgetting is to continue with *distributed practice*. This means that after your first learning period, when you used multiple repetitions to learn the material, you quickly go through the list again in your head (or better you say it, or write it down) at intervals of hours, and then days. Even more effective is to try to vary the way in which you do these different repetitions (you could think it, say it, write short notes, diagram it, etc.). This variation can stop you getting into a rut where you are simply repeating without thinking about it. This way of rehearsing memories over time has been shown to be more effective than simply repeating exactly the same thing the same number of times in a single learning session.

I recently read an article in a golf magazine that ended with "Now you have the skill, continue to practise it once a week if possible". This is what is meant by distributed practice.

By a Practice and Check Cycle

However the most effective way to use repetition is to adopt a *Practice and Check Cycle*. This strategy builds distributed practice into a process that ensures that what you practise is always on track. While the way in which you use this strategy will differ slightly, depending on the actual material being learned, the essential features are:

1. Start by looking closely at the word, list, map or paragraph you want to remember. Say it to yourself, either out loud or under your breath. Or write it down. Or think it through. Repeat this several times (*multiple repetitions*) until you feel you know it.

2. Cover up the material.

3. Now write down the word, list, map, poem or concept definition. Or, if that's not possible, say it to yourself, or think it through.

4. Carefully check your response against the original.

If correct

Repeat steps 3 and 4 a few times, preferably at intervals. If you can do this correctly each time, the response should be well fixed in your memory

If incorrect

Pay particular attention to any differences between the correct response and the one you gave. Tell yourself what is wrong and *focus on the differences.*

Then repeat the sequence until you have practised it correctly four or five times in a row with no mistakes.

While the memory should now be fairly well fixed, it can still suffer forgetting if you don't practise it at intervals to gain the benefit of *distributed practice.* And always keep checking you are practising correctly.

Don't be upset if you make mistakes – they are an important part of learning.

Focus closely on the differences between the mistake and what should have happened, and your learning should be greatly improved.

This *Practice and Check Cycle* is important because:

Practice doesn't make perfect.
Only perfect practice makes perfect.

THE STRUCTURING PHASE

While the Structuring Phase is separated here from the Learning Phase, the process of structuring material makes its own big contribution to learning. Structuring involves taking the material to be learned and recasting it into a new format. To do this, the learner has to focus on the material, think about it, and then re-present it in a different form. Usually this different form is a condensed representation of the essential components of the original.

The mental processes involved in structuring material assist learning, and often all a student has to do following the structuring process is a quick check and review of the final representation. The condensed form of the final structure is also more easily recalled when it is needed at a later time.

STRUCTURING NON-MEANINGFUL MATERIAL

When an understanding of the material is impossible (non-meaningful material), rote learning strategies will be adopted. [They might also be adopted for meaningful material if the learner chooses that approach.] Of course the most effective way to store a list of unconnected items is to write them down on paper, or on the hand. These notes can then be referred to when needed. However, while this might be the preferred method for shopping lists, in education students are usually expected to remember specific items without having recourse to a 'paper memory'.

Research evidence shows non-meaningful material is harder to learn than meaningful material, and is more quickly forgotten. Nevertheless there are ways to assist the memory of non-meaningful material that make use of memory strengthening tactics. These memory aids, or mnemonics, can speed up learning, and stabilise memories, by creating artificial linkages (associations), and making use of visualisation. Funnily enough, you will find that many of these strategies seem to increase the amount of material you have to remember, which doesn't seem sensible. Even a simple shopping list of five or six items looks a lot more complicated when it's incorporated into the Method of Place, as you will soon see. Nevertheless, because mnemonics use what the brain is good at doing, the approaches pay off handsomely.

Each of the strategies has its strengths and limitations, and is more effective for particular types of memories. I have selected strategies which are relatively easy to learn, but which can also be quite powerful. Other strategies can be more powerful still, however they take a great deal of time to learn, and require much practice. For instance, I have restricted the pegword approach to 10 words. However expert memorisers will extend the list into the hundreds, and they will also adapt the approach so that each 'peg holder' might hold four or five items. I don't think that level of skill will be required from most readers of this guide, however there are many books and internet sources which will allow you to extend your repertoire if desired.

The different mnemonics introduced are:

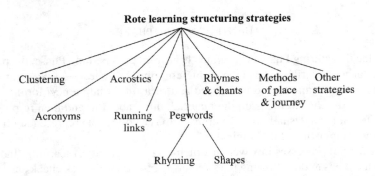

Rote learning structuring strategies

Clustering   Acrostics   Rhymes & chants   Methods of place & journey   Other strategies

Acronyms   Running links   Pegwords

Rhyming   Shapes

One easy way to remember that you have something to remember.

Clustering

Surprisingly, if you are given a long list of items or words to remember, it's easier if you can first divide the list up into several categories, with four or five items in each. How this can work is demonstrated in the memory training approach called Kim's game, which Baden Powell modified from Rudyard Kipling's book *Kim* for use by the Boy Scout movement. A number of articles (25 or so) are placed on a tray then covered. The cover is lifted for about two minutes, and observers are to remember as many articles as possible. I recently used this with students, then asked the successful ones what tactics they had adopted. All of them had used a clustering approach. For instance, one might have mentally clustered together a pen, a ruler, a calculator and an eraser as office supplies. Another student might have used colour for different clusters. One student used 'metal objects', 'plastic objects', etc., for different clusters.

While different clusters were chosen by each individual, the method always worked. This means that any list of unlinked items you need to remember can often be split up into this sort of artificial grouping, and this helps both memorisation and later recall of the information.

As an example, let's say you have a shopping list of: eggs, meat, vegetables, bread, juice, soap, pasta and milk. The easiest way to avoid memorisation is write the list down, but if you can't do this, how can you go about remembering it? Clustering might be an answer, and clusters could be formed around food type, the geographical area where items are found in the supermarket, or even an alphabetical arrangement. For instance, in my local supermarket, I could divide it into 6 main areas that I visit in a clockwise order. First the vegetables (1 item), then the refrigerated section (3 items to remember), then the frozen foods (0 items this time), then the breads/cakes (1 item), then the first half of the shelves (1 item – pasta), and the second half (1 item – soap). That is – 130111. On every visit, I could use the same supermarket geography to jolt my memory of how many items I need to purchase from each section, and that, in its turn, prompts me to think what I need from each.

As a second example, in a science lesson we might need to list, then learn, the skills needed to be a good scientific problem solver. The skills proposed could include about 40 suggestions including the abilities to:

- assemble/construct apparatus
- classify observations
- generate hypotheses
- observe changes
- draw charts and graphs of the results
- identify a problem

To try and put these together, so we can remember them when needed, one way could be to identify clusters of abilities, which might include such things as: problem identifying skills, planning skills, information collecting skills, recording skills, interpreting skills, communicating skills. The planning skills section would then cluster together all items related to planning, for example:

Planning skills

- generating hypotheses
- deciding where to obtain necessary information
- designing appropriate experiments
- ensuring variables are controlled

Other clusters would include related abilities, and this reorganised list would now be much easier to remember than the unclustered original.

Clustering can also be used to remember numbers. So rather than remembering 3692 as three, six, nine, two, you can reduce the demands on memory be changing it to thirty-six, ninety-two. Here you have only two things to remember instead of four. And if you can relate one or both of the numbers to something else – your birthday, etc. – that makes it easier still.

Most people can keep in mind only 5–9 isolated pieces of information. This is why telephone numbers were kept at 7 digits for a long time.

The true art of memory is the art of attention.

Samuel Johnson

Acronyms

In an acronym the first letters of the important elements of a list are remembered by forming an understandable word or phrase. While the items themselves still have to be remembered, the acronym provides a handle that assists retrieval from memory.

The well-known ROY G BIV is used to assist the memory of the colours of the rainbow. The dicarboxylic acids (a chemical term for acids with two -COOH groups) are remembered by OMSGAP (oxalic, malonic, glutaric, succinic, adipic, pimelic). If the order of the elements of the list isn't important, they can be rearranged to make a real word – the Great Lakes of Canada & USA can be remembered through HOMES – Huron, Ontario, Michigan, Erie and Superior. In other cases, when a real word can't be made, you could reorganise the initial letters to form something that looks like a legitimate word, and is also memorable. For instance to remember the characteristics of living things, i.e. they move, respire, are sensitive, grow, reproduce, excrete, and need nutrition, one could use MRS GREN.

In geometry we have the right-angled triangle as below:

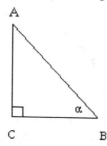

For that triangle the following apply

$$\sin\alpha = \frac{\text{Opposite}}{\text{Hypotenuse}}, \quad \cos\alpha = \frac{\text{Adjacent}}{\text{Hypotenuse}}, \quad \tan\alpha = \frac{\text{Opposite}}{\text{Adjacent}}$$

These are remembered by SOH CAH TOA

DR VANDERSTAMP lists the initial letter of common French verbs conjugated in the passé composé with "être" instead of the standard "avoir": descendre, revenir, venir, aller, naître, devenir, être, retourner, sortir, tomber, arriver, mourir, passer.

SELECKT helps to memorise the forms of energy (Sound, Electrical, Light, Elastic, Chemical, Kinetic, Thermal). And you are probably familiar with acronyms such as LASER (light amplification by stimulated emission of radiation) and SCUBA (self contained underwater breathing apparatus) where the acronym has now become an acceptable word in its own right, and where the full terminology is often unknown. Many workplaces or professions generate a multitude of their own acronyms that are incomprehensible to outsiders.

For practice

Try to rearrange the following shopping list so you can make an acronym to help you remember it.

cereal, eggs, butter, milk, juice, bread, oranges, soup

Sometimes there are alternatives. WASP-LEG assists memory of the classical seven deadly sins (wrath, avarice, sloth, pride, lust, envy and gluttony), but there are other ways of ordering the letters. Try to make one or two other memorable acronyms for these same sins.

Acrostics

These are phrases or sentences which, like acronyms, remind the learner of the first letter of the important words. Assuming you have learned the important words quite well, but have a little difficulty in recalling them, especially recalling them in a particular order, an acrostic might help. Knowing the first letter will usually act as a trigger or prompt to the actual word.

Richard of York gave Battle in Vain gives the first letter of the colours of the rainbow. And the lines of the treble clef are remembered by Every Good Boy Deserves Fruit or Every Guitarist Begins Doing Fine. Often you can invent your own to help you remember the first letter of the components of a list. Interestingly, the emergency call SOS was introduced because of the ease of transmitting it in Morse code: ...- - -.... However "Save Our Souls" is frequently used to aid its memory.

Cuddly-Garfield Tastes-Ants represents the pairing of bases in DNA (cytosine pairs with guanine, and thymine with adenine).

To remember musical key signatures. For fifths, Charlie Goes Down And Enters Bottle-shop For Christmas, and for fourths, Fly BEA Direct Gatwick Central. The open strings of a guitar can be recalled through Elephants And Deadly Gators Break Eggs (this was originally devised by a primary school student).

For the biologist, the order of teeth (incisors, canines, premolars, molars) is seen in I Can Play Marbles.

And the chemical halogen elements (fluorine, chlorine, bromine, iodine) are retained by First Come Back Inside.

The passage of air into the lungs is through the nose or mouth, into the trachea or windpipe, then the bronchi, bronchioles and alveoli.

No Milk

Today With

Bill

Bloggs

Away

For the planets, in order from the sun, we have:

My Very Easy Method Just Speeds Up Naming Planets
(Mercury, Venus, Earth, Mars, Jupiter, Saturn, Uranus, Neptune, Pluto).

And for the order of the balls to be potted after all the reds in snooker:

You Go Brown Before Potting Black
(Yellow, Green, Brown, Blue, Pink, Black)

Acrostics can also help with remembering car number plates. So my WWB073 becomes "Willie Wonka's Breakfast 073".

When you have a list to remember, see if you can generate an acrostic. For instance, let's imagine that this afternoon I must visit the bank, collect some photographs, return a book to the library, and then go to the supermarket. So we have

B, P, L, S – or Big Pigs Like Singing. Shopping lists can be remembered, and their retrieval helped, in the same way.

In the classroom, individual students, or the class as a whole, can generate an acrostic that has a particular meaning for them.

For practice

Try to make up an acrostic for the following:

1. The bones associated with the human arm – scapula, clavicle, humerus, ulna, radius, carpals, metacarpals, phalanges.
2. The New England states of the United States – Maine, Vermont, New Hampshire, Rhode Island, Connecticut and Massachusetts.

Rhymes, Chants and Phrases

These can be very helpful, and below are some common ones. Sometimes it's possible to make up your own quite quickly, but they are not normally very useful strategies for general use.

"*In 1492 Columbus sailed the ocean blue*" sticks in the memory, and "*30 days has September ...*" reminds us of the lengths of the months. In the same vein: "*When the mites go up, the tights come down*" tells us that stalagmites build from the ground, and stalactites hang from the roof. And psychology students wishing to remember stages of Freud's personality theory will be aware of "*Id the kid*".

In more lengthy rhymes and chants we are creating artificial associations, or linkages, between different bits of information. We are also using the tactic known as *chunking* (see Part 1); that is placing a lot of information together in one lump, so making the total amount easier to remember. As an illustration of the value of this, note how we can say the alphabet easily if we start at A – but it's a little bit harder if we have to begin at K. And it's more difficult still if we have to repeat it backwards. Because of the many times we've rehearsed it, it has become bound together as a single chunk of information. Of course, we can break this down and start at K, but we have to think a little before we start. This also applies if we try to start a well-known prayer or poem partway through. Similarly, if young piano players make a mistake in a piece they are playing, they often have to restart from the beginning. The whole piece has been learned as one chunk – each part follows automatically.

Here are some other examples:

For treating shock
   If the face is red, raise the head; if the face is pale, raise the tail.

For correct punctuation
   It's always right to use an apostrophe when shortening it is, but never for its own sake.

For turning screws
> *Lefty loosey, righty tighty*

To assist spelling
> *i before e, except after c.*

> *There is a LIE in believe*
> *There's an ACHE in every teacher*

For some historical dates
> *In fourteen hundred and ninety two, Columbus sailed the ocean blue*

> *In sixteen hundred and sixty-six, London burned like a pile of sticks*

> *In nineteen hundred and three, the brothers Wright flew free*

What happened to Henry 8th's six wives?
> *Divorced, beheaded, died; divorced, beheaded, survived.*

The English monarchs from 1066
> *Willy, Willy, Harry, Ste(ve)*
> *Harry, Dick, John, Harry 3.*
> *Edward 1,2,3, Dick 2,*
> *Henry 4,5,6, then who? Edward 4,5, Dick the Bad,*
> *Harry's twain, then Ned the Lad.*
> *Mary, Lizzie, James you ken, Charlie, Charlie, James again.*
> *William & Mary, Anne O'Gloria,*
> *4 Georges, William and Victoria.*
> *Edward 7 and George 5,*
> *Edward, George and Liz alive.*

Some of us remember the names of the elements of the chemical periodic table using a chant. And a Monty Python song outlines our place in the universe.

> *"Just remember that you're standing on a planet that's evolving*
> *And revolving at nine hundred miles an hour*
> *It's orbiting at nineteen miles a second, so it's reckoned,*
> *'Round the sun that is the source of all our power ...."*

Again, just as you would if you were learning a piano piece or a poem, you follow the initial rehearsal steps then adopt the *Practice and Check Cycle* to memorise.

Visualisations, Associations and Running Links

> Strategies that generate visualisations and associations are particularly effective.

All of these strategies involve making links, or associations, between something you want to learn, and something you already know. The links can be sound, image or word related – or a mixture of these.

Recently I was introduced to man called Harvey, a name I found difficult to remember. He had a wisp of grey hair that reminded me of Harvey the rabbit, a character in a TV show. Now, with this visualised image and its rabbit *association*, I have no problem with his name. (Further on some suggestions are made to help with the memory of names.)

Associations can also be made in the educational setting. For instance, for remembering some German vocabulary and pronunciation:

die Leute (= people)
   Picture a crowd of people 'loitering' in the street
kaum (= hardly/scarcely)
   Hear a broad southern U.S. accent saying to a friend, "You hardly come to see me these days".

I developed a *running link* (a continuous set of individual images linked together) to remember the planets in the correct order from the sun. It starts with a pool of silver coloured mercury on the ground. Along comes Venus (with long blond hair), picks some up and throws it, splat, at the earth. From the splat arises a very large, green Martian exclaiming, "By Jupiter, I've just sat down (Saturn) hard on my behind (Uranus) and I can't get up". Just then along comes Neptune, trident and all, dragging behind his spotted dog Pluto, and they manage to pull him up.

This has worked very well for me. I created the links between the planets, and formed a single chunk, full of associations and visualisations. After only three practices I could remember the list accurately. Even though I added additional material, the new structure made learning much more efficient.

One problem with running links is that if a step is missed, there is nothing in the method that tells you this (as opposed, for instance, to the Journey method). However for short lists, they are very useful.

If you use them, here are some useful hints:

- adopt pleasant images
- create vivid images (bright colours, noisy, smelly etc.)
- exaggerate the size of important parts of the image
- give your image three dimensions and movement
- use humour! Funny or peculiar things are easier to remember. Rude images and links are particularly difficult to forget!

31

Finally use the *Practice and Check Cycle* to help you memorise.

For practice

> Try to generate a running link for the counties in the south of England – Avon, Dorset, Somerset, Cornwall, Wiltshire, Devon, Gloucestershire, Hampshire, and Surrey.
>
> To start you off:
> An AVON (Avon) lady is knocking on a heavy oak DOoR (Dorset). The DOoR opens to show a beautiful SuMmER landscape with a SETting sun (Somerset).

Pegwords

This strategy helps you to remember lists. First you remember a list of pegwords to represent numbers. Later you attach your list to these. There are different types of pegwords including rhyming and shape related ones. A suitable list of words rhyming with the numbers 1–10 can be taken from the traditional children's song *Knick knack paddy whack*:

1. Drum
2. Shoe
3. Tree
4. Door
5. Hive
6. Sticks
7. Heaven
8. Gate
9. Line
10. Hen

If you know the song, you have the pegwords for the first ten items on your list. You then create strong visual images linking your list words to the pegwords. For the planets you might start with a large blue drum laid on its end, with globules of silver mercury rolling backward and forward all over it. This is followed by Venus, long fair hair blowing in the wind, standing in a very large shoe; and then a forest of tall pine trees sticking out of the earth, and so on. If you can link images together, creating a sort of story, so much the better.

Another set of pegwords uses a picture relationship:

1. Pen
2. Swan
3. Bird in flight
4. Sailboat
5. Hook
6. Golf club
7. Cliff

8. Snowman
9. Lollipop
10. Bat and ball

You should see a resemblance between the shape of the number and the related pegword. These can then be used like the previous list. For instance as we begin by writing using a long pen being dipped in mercury, Venus enters sitting on a white swan and so on.

One advantage of pegwords is that the learner can jump immediately to any place in the list without working right through the list from the beginning. The question, *What is the fifth planet from the Sun?* immediately prompts five and you jump to Hive (or hook) and to the visualisation you have created linking Jupiter to your pegword.

The pegword list can be extended in two ways. Memory experts might use a list of up to 100 pegwords, though an alternative is to use one pegword to store several items together. For instance, if a shopping list begins with: bread, orange juice, washing powder and bananas, you could create a visual image linking these four to drum (i.e. one) in a single image. There is a large red drum, and sitting on it is a chimpanzee with a bread roll in one hand, and a banana in the other, banging furiously. From one side of the drum there is an oozing of soapsuds, from the other side orange juice pours out. It doesn't matter how silly the image is – in fact the sillier the better. Construct it in your mind; then strongly imagine the total image (don't bother to think of the actual words you have to remember – stick with the image). This should fix the list in your memory very quickly. Now your next few items of your shopping list can be attached to shoe (two).

For a detailed look at the pegword approach, and a step-by-step sequence of how to use it, see Pease and Pease (1992).

For practice

> Your shopping list consists of milk, bread, cornflakes, bananas and jam. Make up five images to link each, in turn, to the first five pegwords. As a starter you could have a large drum, pushed over on its side, with several cartons of milk on top.

Methods of Place and Journey

These two strategies are quite similar, and are favourites of memory champions who use them to remember a vast amount of information. Both have an inbuilt structure, which combine the best aspects of both running links and pegwords. This ensures you construct memorable images, but also that you can proceed logically through your list, without missing an item. This makes both strategies flexible and very powerful.

In the Method of Place, you choose a familiar place (for example your home, your church or school, etc.). In that place you identify as many memorable positions as there are objects to remember, and then you form a concrete picture of each item on your list, one by one, at the positions. So, for the planets, by the table in your hall you imagine a pool of mercury. As you move down the hall, you see Venus coming out of the dining room – and so on. Or you can do exactly the same thing with the items on your shopping list.

This mnemonic can be used for both short term and long term remembering. So, for remembering things you need for only a short time, you can reserve one place, and a number of positions in it. For instance I could keep my lounge room only for shopping lists. In it I will identify 15 places, which I can use to associate the different items in my list. For instance, in the corner by the CD player, I imagine an orange tree, packed with fruit (reminding me to buy orange juice), and so on round the room. After the visit to the supermarket, the list can be mentally wiped, and the same positions used again for a new list on the next occasion. Of course, if you have fewer than 15 items, only use the first few positions.

For longer term memories, the place, and its positions, need to be maintained, so you need to use a different place, with different positions, that you are not going to reuse for anything else.

The Journey System is a similar strategy using a trip instead of one place. Again it makes use of visual associations, where the list is tied to particular positions in a journey you are familiar with. In my case I associated items on a shopping list to positions that are significant in my walk to the nearby main road.

The list was: milk, bread, coffee, vegetables, detergent, orange juice, soup, razor blades, meat, eggs.

> Front door: right by the front door is a spilled pool of milk all over the expensive brightly coloured rug
>
> Gate: hanging from the gatepost is a loaf of bread with a large number of giant pink mice jumping to reach it
>
> Coffee shop: of course, bags and bags of coffee
>
> Memorial Garden: extra large vegetables of all types scattered through the garden
>
> Old Council Chambers: froths of foam are seeping out under the door and right down the street
>
> Hotel: glass after glass of orange juice on the bar, but no beer
>
> Aviary: all colours of budgies are splashing in a giant soup bowl
>
> Post Office: there are several sacks of mail on the floor, and I am partway through slitting the envelopes open using a large razor
>
> Bric-a-Brac shop: just inside the door there's a black and white steer walking around saying "please buy me and chop a bit off to eat"
>
> Old Registry Building: decorating the front of the building are coloured eggs, big ones and small ones all tied together, and some with coloured chicks breaking out

As with the Method of Place, you can maintain a shopping list journey, which can be used, wiped and reused. But you can also have other journeys for material that has to be remembered for a longer time.

Importantly, for both these methods, make sure you have a very clear idea of the place or journey you intend to use, and its relevant positions before you try to memorise. Then you can simply visualise a strong image at each of the positions.

> Make your images as extravagant and as funny as you can. If possible, relate them to your own interests or experiences. Use size, colour, sound and smell to make each one memorable.

Other Strategies

Some aids-to-memory can't easily be classified, because they are used for only a single memory task. For instance putting your two sets of knuckles together can help you remember which are the long months (31 days) and short months.

And you can invent your own. For instance, recently a new planetoid, named Sedna, was discovered in our solar system. I found this a difficult name to remember. However, once I saw it is Andes in reverse, it became easy. So look for tricks like this.

Even telephone numbers can be remembered by giving them some sort of association. In my area of Australia, South Australia always begins with 8, and Victor Harbor is always 552, so anyone in Victor Harbor begins 8552, and I don't have to remember this separately for everyone I know. So I really only have to learn four digits for each person, not eight. And these four digits are easier learned as two pairs – 8435 becomes eighty-four thirty-five.

A soldier in the First World War bet another that he could get him to memorise the gender of a hundred French words in under a minute. When challenged, he replied "All words ending in 'tion' (e.g. action, fonction, absorption) are feminine".

> Help your memory by using any tricks you can to make connections.

In Summary

All these strategies are effective, so choose the ones you feel happiest with. Some, such as the method of place, are very old, and are used to remember vast lists by expert memorisers. All of them handle material in a way that takes account of the brain's potential to retain information most efficiently when it is linked together through such things as words and images.

If you want to learn some specific un-linked information, use one of the strategies above to help you make links.

But do it fairly quickly. Don't waste more time than you save.

From *New Scientist*, 2005, 2511 (6th August), p. 56:

Last week, one of the New Scientist's medical correspondents had an appointment to interview a scientist who works on combatting memory loss. Sadly, though he didn't turn up. The reason? He forgot.

SOME EVERYDAY MEMORY CHALLENGES

Many of the memory challenges we face daily are related to faces and names, numbers (e.g. telephone numbers and PINs), and lists (e.g. shopping lists and lists of things to do). For the most part, none of the individual items have any meaning attached to them, nor are they connected to other items. However, there are several possibilities for assisting our memories of such things. The obvious one is to write them down, on paper or on the hand, but this is not always convenient.

My granddaughter, Suzannah, aged 7, made her list.

A second way is to keep them in mind by simple rehearsal (that is you keep saying them to yourself). This can work for a short while with such things as telephone numbers (providing you are not distracted), but it is more effective to make use of one of the mnemonics described earlier. Some strategies which can be used for different purposes are outlined below.

You will need to refer to other parts of this guide to see details of how strategies are used. Practise with a new strategy until you can use it easily and effectively. Then keep using it occasionally.

Names Remembering names, or at least retrieving them from memory, can be a problem for many people. While you recognise someone, there is no obvious way that their name is associated with their appearance. To aid memory of names, repetition is important, so when you are introduced, try to say the name again immediately – "Pleased to meet you, Jack!", then use it again in conversation occasionally (most people like their name being used). Another way is to demonstrate interest in the name saying things like – "Elliott" – is that with one t or two?", or "Winton – any relation to the author, Tim Winton?".

Alternatively, try to make a link between the name and the face by creating mental images. When you are introduced, discreetly identify an unusual feature – ears, hair, eyebrows, eyes, nose, mouth, or chin. Then *visualise* an association between that characteristic, the person's face, and the name in your mind. Or you can try to tie the name in with another person you know with the same name, and imagine the two faces together. Or associate the face, or a defining feature, with a unique, but relevant, image - for instance Rosemary is easy. One might imagine her with a gambolling lamb (rosemary is used with lamb roasts).

> If you remember my name, you pay me a subtle compliment; you indicate that I have made an impression on you. Remember my name and you add to my feeling of importance.
>
> Dale Carnegie

Numbers Sometimes it is possible to build some slight 'meaning' into telephone numbers. For instance if a person lives in Myrtle Bank, on the outskirts of Adelaide, the probability is that the number will start with 8379. So, because I am aware of this, I won't have to generate a specific link for it.

Assume the number to be remembered is 8379 2648. I already have the first four numbers, so all I have left is 2648. The first step is to see whether this has any potential meaning for you – does it relate in any way to family birth dates, etc.? If so, then images can be generated to tie the owner of the telephone number to that meaning. An alternative is to make things easier by clustering the numbers – chanting twenty-six, forty-eight should be easier than remembering two, six, four eight.

If you can't use either of these, a combination of pegwords with the Journey or Place strategy is useful. The rhyming pegwords for 2648 are shoe, sticks, door and gate. So, starting your journey at the front door, there is a big pile of shoes. Next to the gate (position 2) someone has constructed a rickety arbour of sticks. On the next corner (position 3), a very large cathedral type wooden door has been propped. Then at position 4, the road is blocked by a level crossing type gate with flashing lights.

Lists Several of the different mnemonics can be used to remember lists, though the strategy selected will depend on the length of the list.

Relatively short lists respond well to the running link strategy. The problem with this approach, that it allows you to drop items out without providing you with any hint that you have done so, is not too important with a short list – however it does mean the strategy has its limits. Also useful for short lists are the two pegword approaches.

For longer lists, it might be possible to form small (4–6 items) sub-groups using a clustering approach, especially if the order in which you have to remember the items is not important. Alternatively, the journey or pegword strategies can be used, as both provide for remembering a number of items in a fixed order.

> Make sure your mnemonic uses vivid images, and run it through a few times in your mind, focussing on the images.

STRUCTURING MEANINGFUL MATERIAL

When structuring potentially meaningful information for memorisation, such as a section of textbook, the trick is to take advantage of the fact that the links are naturally there. Unlike learning un-linked material, they don't have to be created.

The key is to process material by identifying and recording important ideas and internal connections and, as far as you can, by linking its content to what you already know. This sort of *elaborate processing* is the most important tactic you can adopt when you want to memorise this type of material. What it means is that you have to read the material carefully, think about what it means, and then represent it in a different, and condensed form. The mental activity involved in going through this process is, by itself, almost enough to guarantee that the material won't be forgotten. As insurance though, adoption of the *Practice and Check Cycle* (see Section "The Learning Phase" in the beginning of Part 3) should ensure success.

Once the links are identified, how you create a memory that represents the structure of the information will depend on your preferred structuring strategy. While the emphasis in this guide is on assisting memory, you will soon see that most of the strategies can also be contributors to the effective study of new material. So, whether you are trying to learn a scientific theory, a political interpretation, a poem or a novel, you will find at least one of the strategies below will be helpful.

Meaningful information consists of a web of ideas or concepts that are linked to other ideas or concepts. Importantly, a concept is a generalisation in a person's mind which only gets its meaning from its relationships with other concepts in the mind. A chair is part of furniture, but it differs from a table (even though you can sit on a table!) and other classes of furniture. In your mind it might link to wood, but it also links to metal, plastic and so on. It's linked to the concept of sitting, and to the concept of person, and to the number one (one person usually sits on a chair). And so on. It is these sorts of relationships that we can try to summarise in various ways so that the material is organised in preparation for learning.

Most of the strategies below (in fact all apart from the word-based SQ3R) use diagrams to represent the concepts, or main ideas, and the relationships between them. Some learners are uncomfortable with this, and for them a word-based approach is preferred. If that's you, SQ3R, or some modification, is the way to go. And this may also be the method of choice for others when the material does not lend itself easily to diagrammatic representation. For those who like diagrams, there are many possibilities. Depending on the type of information you are summarising, you might find one form is better than the others. The real point is that how you organise new material, and how you summarise it in diagram form, is really up to you – there are no fixed rules.

All the approaches given here are tried and tested, and you will probably always find one that will help you with any particular material. Hopefully, at least one of them will be able to take you beyond the stage where "it may be tempting to resign oneself to the inefficient process of repetitively reading the information in the hope that it will eventually be memorised" (Jones, 2003).

Because the purpose of this guide is to help you memorise, none of the strategies is set in concrete. Any of them can be modified if it helps **YOU** to remember. However the guidelines below apply to anything you do.

All strategies require you to:

- study the information carefully and identify the important ideas
- organise these ideas into a structured form
- relate the information to what you already know

These steps will help you to understand the material, and create linked and lasting memories of it.

After the structuring step, usually little else is needed to support memory; because once the material is elaborated and structured it can often be remembered very well. But it is usually best to follow-up with the *Practice and Check Cycle*. Details of how you can go about this are shown only after the hierarchical concept map section. However, this same general approach will be the same for all the strategies, though minor modifications may be needed.

The strategies for structuring meaningful material introduced in this section are:

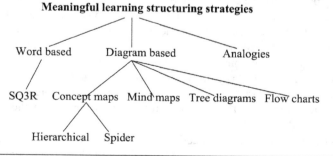

Meaningful learning structuring strategies

Word based   Diagram based   Analogies

SQ3R   Concept maps   Mind maps   Tree diagrams   Flow charts

Hierarchical   Spider

The true art of memory is the art of attention.

Samuel Johnson

SQ3R

This is a powerful approach to extracting and organising the important information from text or other material. By itself, it produces condensed, structured notes. However its power can be enhanced by supplementing it with other strategies, such as mind maps, which help organise the notes diagrammatically, and allow you to make use of other memory strengthening tactics. The effect of SQ3R is to make the time you spend studying a document or text more beneficial, and make your memory of it more permanent. The acts of raising questions, and of seeking answers to them, contribute to the elaborate processing and structuring of the material, both key factors in the formation of long-term memories.

When presented with text, the SQ3R strategy involves five steps:

1. Survey
2. Question
3. Read
4. Recall
5. Review

To apply it to a document, a chapter of a textbook, or even a short paragraph, the approach is the same.

- *Survey*. The first step is to scan the text quickly. Often the first and last sentences of a paragraph give a good idea of what it's about. For a longer document skim through it paying attention to the list of contents, any introduction, the headings of sub-sections, the introductions and summaries to each chapter or section, and any final summary. Does the material seem as though it will be useful? If so, proceed to the next steps; if not discard it.
- *Question*. Jot down a list of any questions that your survey raised. How does it fit with what you already know? What else do you need to know about? Possibly it will be useful to quickly scan the document again at this stage to see whether the questions are addressed. These questions can serve as a device for structuring the content of the document in your own mind.
- *Read* the material carefully with your questions in mind. Concentrate carefully on any parts you have difficulty understanding and make notes. This will often be the slowest step, and you will need to ensure you understand the information, and keep a written record of the important points. If you are happy with diagrams, you may wish to draw a mind map to help you sort out the important points, and their relationship to each other.
- *Recall* the material. Put your notes on one side, and try to run through the content and structure. If you have difficulty, check your notes, then try again. Repeat this step several times (it doesn't take very long) to fix the information in your mind.
- *Review*. Here you need to practise using the material (in effect this should be a *Practice and Check Cycle*). You could re-read the document, and try to relate it to your notes, expanding these where they are too sparse. Or you could discuss the material with other students. Make any changes necessary,

and then repeat these last two steps.

> Material that is well understood is more easily memorised, and more easily recalled when needed.

Hierarchical Concept Maps

The notion of hierarchical concept mapping was developed in the 1960s at Cornell University by Joe Novak, and was based on the learning theory of David Ausubel who stressed the importance of linking new learning into the network of what is already known.

Essentially concept maps are a means of representing knowledge in pictorial form, with the diagrams being representations of a network of concepts held in a person's mind. Importantly, they can be small or big. A whole topic can be mapped, or just a small part of it.

The map below shows a typical map constructed from the content of one page of a science textbook.

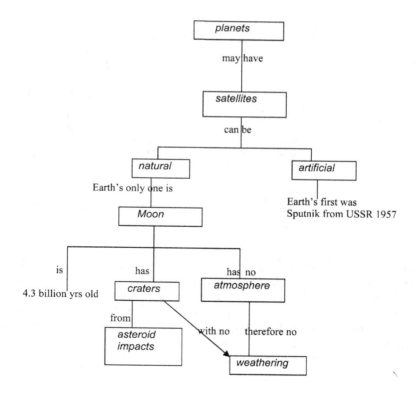

The map shows the main concepts in the material (these are placed in rectangles), and the links between them. Exactly how concepts relate to each other is indicated by labelling each link. As far as possible the maps are hierarchically organised. That is, the most inclusive or general concept is at the top, with the map radiating down to more specific concepts. Specific information or examples can be added, though not within rectangles which hold concepts (i.e. generalisations) only.

A different example below shows the types of plants in different forest areas of the western U.S. Notice that the links are not labelled, however my view is that this makes it less useful as an aid to memory than when the relationship between each pair of concepts is shown.

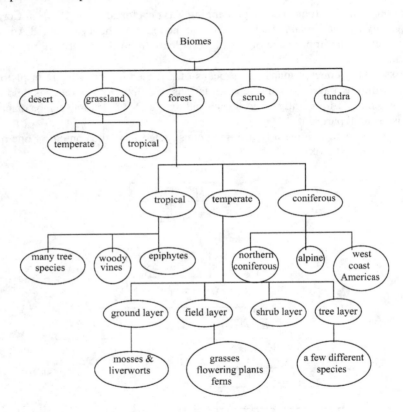

Developing this hierarchical structure is often difficult, and the hierarchy doesn't matter too much so long as the structure you create helps you remember. Generally though, the topic which is of major interest to you (e.g. the topic of a chapter or paragraph) will be at the top, with links down to other concepts. It is also true that a neat, more structured, map like the one above is easier to remember than a hotch-potch of concepts with links running in all directions.

Let's look at the formation of a simple map derived from a typical paragraph, or chapter, of text.

1. Identify the major concepts related to the topic. Remember that you decide what concepts to put in to best organise your understanding, so you can add to the concepts in the text from your own knowledge if this helps. To help memory, you probably don't want more than 12–15 concepts in a map, so split the topic if necessary.
2. Write each concept on a different scrap of paper.
3. Move them around on the table to try to best represent the relationships you see between them.
4. Draw the resulting map putting in, and labelling, the links. These labels are important as they indicate how you perceive the actual relationship between each pair of concepts.
5. Identify any other links, including any cross-links, which can relate together different parts of your map. The ability to see these relationships is a sign of a sound understanding of the topic.

(Note the initial letters of these steps can be remembered by the acrostic: I Want My Dinner Immediately.)

After constructing the map, your memory of it should be fairly good. To be sure though, adopt some form of the *Practice and Check Cycle*. For instance you could:

1. look at the shape of your map, and at each concept and its relationship to others
2. explain to yourself why you wrote what you did (i.e. make sure you remember why you linked concepts in particular ways)
3. cover the map or close your eyes and try to picture it in your mind
4. with the original covered, try to redraw the map and write in both the concepts and links (it doesn't have to be drawn in exactly the same way, but it should pick up the same important concepts and links)
5. check to see where you were right, and where you missed sections or drew inappropriate links
6. if you made errors, look closely at the map again, and particularly at the places where you made the errors. Carefully focus on the differences between the correct and incorrect versions.
7. cover, and sketch it again
8. a couple of repeats should be enough to fix it firmly into memory

---

Note that there is no single correct map. You are constructing them for your own purpose. That is to help **you** remember connections.

The more connections that can be made in the brain, the more integrated the experience is within memory.

Don Campbell

Spider Concept Maps

Rather than the top down approach in the hierarchical concept maps, spider concept maps place the main concept in the centre. Because the formal structure is not so rigid, I find them easier to construct. Around the central concept are linked the various main concepts you have identified, and around each of these other more specific concepts are inserted, followed by specific examples. Typical structures are shown below, and again it is helpful if the links are labelled.

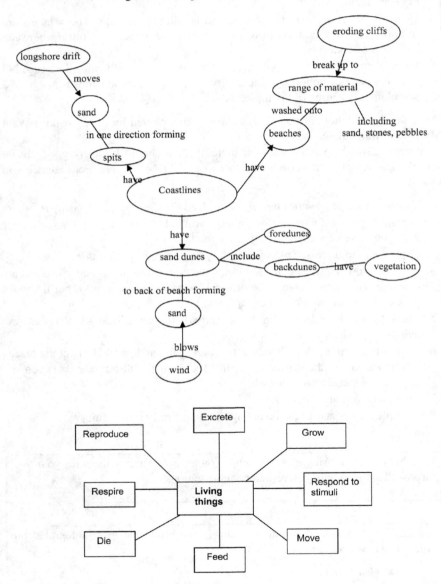

For practice

> Try drawing a map for the paragraph below.
>
> The word 'depression' is used in different ways. There is a mild form we can feel on Monday morning, when it's time for school or work. There is also a more severe form that could arise after we have been rejected for a number of jobs. In both of these cases, we know why we feel 'down', though we might not be able to do much about it. In addition to these, there is clinical depression. This is a psychological state for which there seems to be no real reason from within the person's life. A person might appear to have everything in life, and yet is crushed by an uncontrollable burden. The condition seems to be caused by an imbalance in the usual chemicals that control the nervous system. A sufferer might wrestle with the condition for years, however there are now various treatments and drugs which can help.

Mind Maps

These were developed in the 1960s by Tony Buzan in the UK. Like concept maps they provide a means for organising information and the relationships between ideas. However they don't focus specifically on concepts, and any relevant ideas can be included.

Your map can be any shape that evolves. The important thing is that it should include all the ideas and examples you want to remember, and the links between them. You can include diagrams or pictures if you wish, and use different colours to quickly distinguish the sub-themes.

The two examples summarise information from a school text.

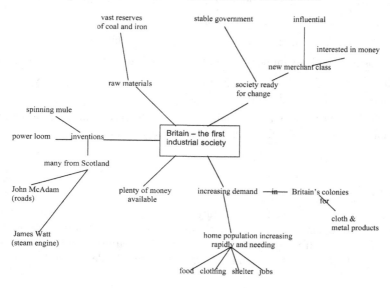

45

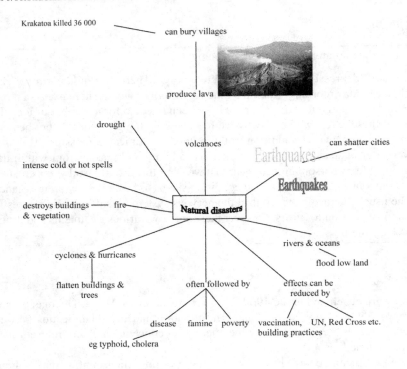

To construct a mind map:

1. identify the main theme and draw circle or rectangle around it.
2. locate the main sub-themes and connect each to the title.
3. find any additional levels and connect each to the sub-theme.
4. identify specific examples which illustrate each sub-theme, and connect them.
5. look at your final map and draw in additional lines to indicate any clear links between different sub-themes or examples.
6. add any other relevant information you already know, but is not found in the material you are studying (e.g. I added "drought" above).

Tree Diagrams

These are particularly useful for sorting out the events and relationships within a novel, play or poem, and for such things as the sequence of historical events.

To the central tree structure you attach branches illustrating the major ideas. Then to each of these you add smaller branches with sub-ideas, and then examples.

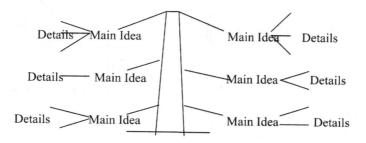

The tree diagram below illustrates some of the history of soldiers who returned to South Australia following the First World War to find themselves jobless. Sometimes, the tree format can be used as a timeline with the beginnings at the bottom, and changes recorded further up the trunk (this is seen in the diagram below).

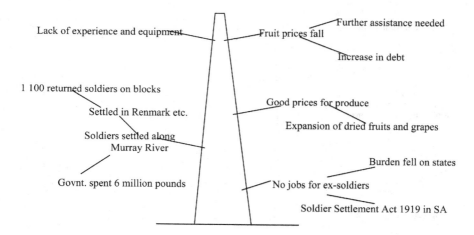

The following diagram summarises the significant historical events in the process of determining the structure of atoms.

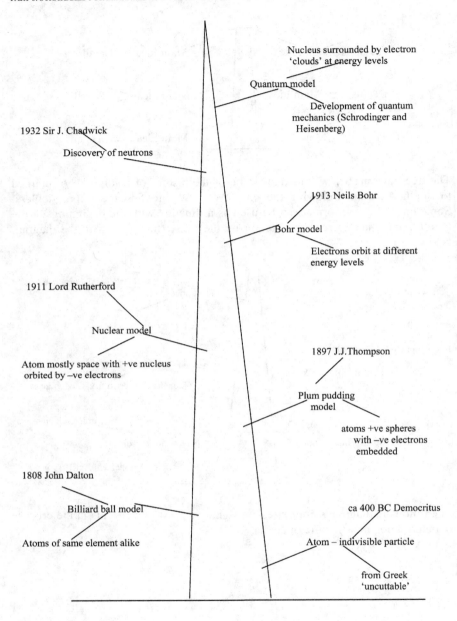

Nucleus surrounded by electron 'clouds' at energy levels

Quantum model

Development of quantum mechanics (Schrodinger and Heisenberg)

1932 Sir J. Chadwick

Discovery of neutrons

1913 Neils Bohr

Bohr model

Electrons orbit at different energy levels

1911 Lord Rutherford

Nuclear model

Atom mostly space with +ve nucleus orbited by −ve electrons

1897 J.J.Thompson

Plum pudding model

atoms +ve spheres with −ve electrons embedded

1808 John Dalton

Billiard ball model

ca 400 BC Democritus

Atoms of same element alike

Atom − indivisible particle

from Greek 'uncuttable'

Flow Charts

A flow chart can usefully summarise a set of events taking place over time. They are used a great deal when considering problem solving and management structures, and in that form the presentation is quite formal, with the following icons being used:

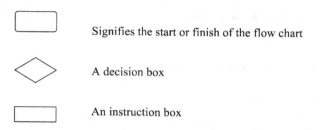

Signifies the start or finish of the flow chart

A decision box

An instruction box

The small flow chart below shows what your early morning preparation for school or work might be like.

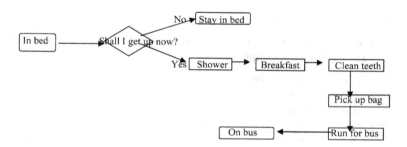

This formal approach is quite appropriate when looking at people making decisions and following instructions, however its use is not necessary for recording all changes. Thus a short geological flow chart might look at the formation, and recycling, of different rock types.

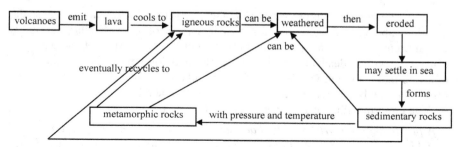

The important thing is for you to design the chart so that it helps you commit the process to memory, and aids your recall when you need it. This means you can structure the chart in any way you wish. For instance, taking a small section of the flowchart above, you can add to it to include actual examples.

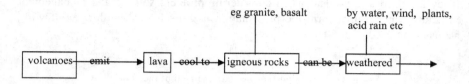

Then remember to use the *Practice and Check Cycle.*

For practice

> Either extend the first flow chart to include decisions made later in the day, or devise a chart related to an everyday activity such as one of the following: doing the washing, planning your last holiday, or planning an afternoon of gardening.

Analogies

Analogies are frequently used to help learners understand and remember difficult concepts. Analogies can be simply stated:

> DNA is like a spiral staircase
> Nuclear reactions are like falling dominoes
> The camera is like the eye
> The earth's crust is like that of a peach
> God is like a shepherd

But analogies can be more complex. For instance several similarities between the flow of electricity and the pumping of water are often drawn. Also, there are some similarities between what a doctor can do to find out what is going on inside your body, and how geologists study the inside of the earth. In all these cases though, we have to be careful.

Analogies are helpful for memory, but they can ruin understanding. Because the two things being compared are not identical, some aspects are similar, but others are different. And it's important that you distinguish between these. Otherwise you can get the wrong idea by assuming similarities that don't exist. As an example: at times, to make a point, we say that atoms are like miniature billiard balls. In one respect, it may be so, but in most ways atoms are not at all like billiard balls.

The important thing is to use analogies if they help you remember

A public health instructor, who had been helping new parents to care for their babies, recounted one analogy. As the way of wrapping the infant was being demonstrated, a young Asian couple turned and asked, "You mean we should wrap the baby like an egg roll". "Yes", said the instructor "that's a good analogy".

50

"I don't know how to make egg rolls", said another mother anxiously, "can I wrap my baby up like a burrito?"

When learning something new, see if you can see any similarities with something you already know. But be careful about seeing similarities that don't exist.

HOW TO JOG YOUR MEMORY

Despite using all sorts of memory aids to help us store and recall memories, on occasion we have difficulty retrieving something we need. This problem is usually related to semantic or autobiographical memory, though on one occasion I totally forgot how to tie my tie (procedural knowledge). For two days, my wife tied it for me (most embarrassing!), but then the memory returned. So what does one do when a memory won't come?

1. Try to think about the occasion when you learned it, and the circumstances. Sometimes that will serve as a trigger.
2. If the object was a part of a list, try to remember some other items on the list, to see if that jolts retrieval.
3. If you can think of the general context of what you learned, and its purpose and relationship to other things, that might help.
4. If all that fails, try not to worry about it. Just forget about trying to remember, and move on to something else. Often the thing you want leaps into your mind in a very short time.

Two perspectives on memory. Together they emphasise its problems.

Do not trust your memory; it is a net full of holes; the most beautiful prizes slip through it.
> Georges Duhamel

Our memories are independent of our wills. It is not so easy to forget.
> Richard Sheridan

A FLOW CHART FOR LEARNING DECISIONS

Ultimately, you decide what you want to learn, and how you will go about it. In doing this, you have choices to make, and these are outlined in the flow chart.

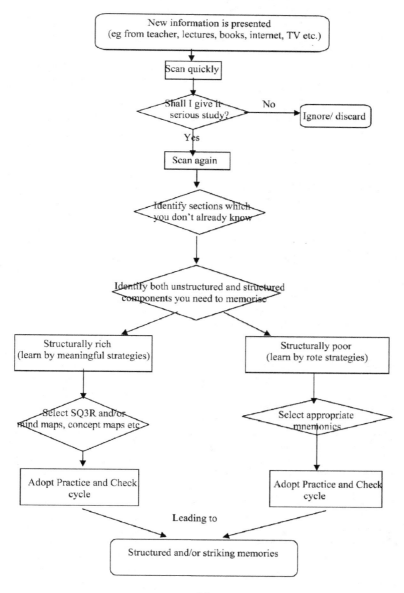

BIBLIOGRAPHY

Borges, J.L. 1962. Funes the memorious. In *Labyrinths. Selected stories and other writings*, D.A. Yates and J.E. Irby (eds.). New York: New Direction Publishing Company.

Buzan, T. and Buzan, B. 2001. *The Mind Map Book*. London: BBC.

Jones, B. 2006. *A Thinking Reed*. Crows Nest, N.S.W.: Allen and Unwin.

Jones, H. 2003. From a Grad. Dip. Ed. Essay on "Learning strategies".

Pease, A. and Pease, B. 1992. *Memory Language*. Sydney: Pease Learning Systems.

INDEX

Chunking, 15, 29
Elaborate processing, 38, 40
Emotions, 12
Forgetting, 18
Interference, 18
Learning
   and emotions, 12
   distributed practice, 22
   educational, 4, 14, 19
   incidental, 13
   intentional, 13
   meaningful, 8, 18
   multiple repetition, 21
   practice and check cycle, 22
   procedural, 4, 9, 16
   rote, 8, 18
   semantic knowledge, 4, 6, 9, 16
   skills, 9
Memory
   autobiographical, 16
   control component, 16
   declarative, 16
   episodic, 16
   keys to, 6
   long-term, 14
   non-declarative, 15
   procedural, 16
   recall, 17
   recognition, 17
   short-term, 15
   temporary store, 16
   working, 15
Mnemonics, 24, 36
Procedural knowledge
   learning, 9
   memory, 16

Printed in the United States
By Bookmasters